ROYAL COURT

Royal Court Theatre presents

THE GOOD FAMILY

by **Joakim Pirinen**
translated by **Gregory Motton**

THE KHOMENKO FAMILY CHRONICLES

by **Natalia Vorozhbit**
translated by **Sasha Dugdale**

First performance at Royal Court Theatre, Jerwood Theatre Upstairs,
Sloane Square, London on 30 November 2007.

THE GOOD FAMILY and THE KHOMENKO FAMILY CHRONICLES are presented as part
of International Playwrights: A Genesis Project.

Media Partner
THE
INDEPENDENT

THE GOOD FAMILY

by **Joakim Pirinen**
translated by **Gregory Motton**

Lena **Daisy Lewis**
Janne **Harry Lloyd**
Eva **Samantha Spiro**
Lasse **Jeremy Swift**

THE KHOMENKO FAMILY CHRONICLES

by **Natalia Vorozhbit**
translated by **Sasha Dugdale**

Lyosha **Lewis Lempereur-Palmer**
Lyuda **Samantha Spiro**
Kostya **Jeremy Swift**

Director **Joe Hill-Gibbins**
Designer **Ultz**
Lighting Designer **Trevor Wallace**
Sound Designer **Ian Dickinson**
Choreographer **Luca Silvestrini**
Assistant Director **Michael Longhurst**
Casting Director **Amy Ball**
Production Manager **Sue Bird**
Stage Managers **Carla Archer, Bryony Milne**
Stage Management Work Placement **Joanna Hinton**
Costume Supervisor **Jackie Orton**

The Royal Court and Stage Management wish to thank the following for their help with this production: Melissa Dunne, Sue Emmas and the Genesis Young Directors Programme at the Young Vic, Fiona Morrell, Arne Pohlmeier, Francesca Seeley, Caroline Steinbeis, Hannah Tyrrell-Pinder.

THE COMPANY

Joakim Pirinen (writer)
(THE GOOD FAMILY)
Joakim was born in Lidingö, just outside of
Stockholm, in 1961. He is of Swedish-Finnish
origin.
Publications include: Nine comic books
(1983-2004), including Socker-Conny (1985)
which was adapted into a play; Den Svenska
Apan (The Swedish Monkey) (2001).
Radio includes: Fåglarnas Underbara Liv
(The Wonderful Life of Birds), Skönhetsmord
(Beauty Murder).
As an artist he exhibits regularly and has
illustrated around twenty books. Joakim is
also a journalist, publisher and maker of
short films.

Natalia Vorozhbit (writer)
(THE KHOMENKO FAMILY CHRONICLES)
Natalia was born in Kiev in the Ukraine and
studied at the Moscow Literary Institute.
Two of her plays, DEMONS and GALKA
MOTALKO, have been staged in Moscow and
in the National Theatre of Latvia. GALKA
MOTALKO has been adapted for screen and
is currently being filmed in Moscow.
Her play, THE GRAINSTORE, written as the
result of a commission from the RSC, will be
staged in the Courtyard Theatre in Stratford
in 2009. THE KHOMENKO FAMILY
CHRONICLES was commissioned jointly by
the Royal Court and the BBC World
Service. It was first performed as a
rehearsed reading as part of SMALL TALK:
BIG PICTURE at the Royal Court in 2006.

Ian Dickinson (sound designer)
For the Royal Court: Rhinoceros, My Child,
The Eleventh Capital, The Seagull,
Krapp's Last Tape, Piano/Forte, Rock 'n' Roll
(& Duke of York's/Broadway), Motortown,
Rainbow Kiss, The Winterling, Alice Trilogy,
Fewer Emergencies, Way to Heaven,
The Woman Before, Stoning Mary (& Drum
Theatre, Plymouth), Breathing Corpses,
Wild East, Dumb Show, Shining City (& Gate,
Dublin), Lucky Dog, Blest Be the Tie
(with Talawa), Ladybird, Notes on Falling
Leaves, Loyal Women, The Sugar Syndrome,
Blood, Playing the Victim (with Told By an
Idiot), Fallout, Flesh Wound, Hitchcock

Blonde (& Lyric), Black Milk,
Crazyblackmuthafuckin'self, Caryl Churchill
Shorts, Push Up, Fucking Games, Herons.
Other theatre includes: King Of Hearts
(Out of Joint); Love and Money (Young Vic);
Much Ado About Nothing (redesign, RSC/
Novello); The Hothouse, Pillars of the
Community (National); A Few Good Men
(Haymarket); Dr Faustus (Chichester Festival
Theatre); The Magic Carpet (Lyric
Hammersmith); Port, As You Like It,
Poor Superman, Martin Yesterday, Fast Food,
Coyote Ugly (Royal Exchange, Manchester);
Night of the Soul (RSC/Barbican); Under the
Curse, Eyes of the Kappa (Gate); Crime &
Punishment in Dalston (Arcola); Search &
Destroy (New End); The Whore's Dream
(RSC/Edinburgh).
Ian is Head of Sound at the Royal Court.

Sasha Dugdale (translator)
(THE KHOMENKO FAMILY CHRONICLES)
Sasha has translated over twenty Russian
plays for The Royal Court, including
Ladybird, Black Milk and Plasticine by Vassily
Sigarev; Terrorism and Playing the Victim by
the Presnyakov Brothers. She is currently
translating The Cherry Orchard for the BBC.
She has published two collections of poetry
and two collections of Russian poetry in
translation.

Joe Hill-Gibbins (director)
For the Royal Court: A Girl in a Car with a
Man, The One with the Oven.
Other theatre includes: A Respectable
Wedding (Young Vic); The Fever (Young Vic in
association with Theatre 503); Under the
Curse (Gate); A Thought in Three Parts
(BAC).
Awards include: Jerwood Young Director's
Award 2003; James Menzies-Kitchin Trust
Young Directors Award 2002; Rose Bruford
Memorial Trust Director's Award 2001.
Joe is an Associate Director at the Young Vic.

Lewis Lempereur-Palmer
Lewis currently attends The Barbara Speake
Stage School.
Theatre includes: The Caucasian Chalk
Circle.

Television includes: Omid Djalli Show, Touch Me I'm Karen Taylor, Star Stories, Time Trumpet, Diggin' It, Garth Marenghi, Hear the Silence.
Film includes: The Disappeared, The Beast in the Heart, The Weekend.

Daisy Lewis
Theatre includes: Silence, Blue Moon Over Poplar, Antigone at Hell's Mouth (NYT); The Good Person of Szechuan (Chelsea); Top Girls (Bryanston Arts Centre).
Television includes: Miss Austen Regrets, After You've Gone, Doctor Who.

Harry Lloyd
Theatre includes: The Sea (Theatre Royal Haymarket in 2008); Bash (Trafalgar Studios); The Comedy of Errors (OUDS tour, Japan).
Television includes: Dr Who, Warriors, Robin Hood, Vital Signs, Holby City, The Bill, Pope Town, M.I.T., Goodbye Mr Chips, David Copperfield.

Michael Longhurst (assistant director)
As director, theatre includes: One in Five (Daring Pairings Festival, Hampstead); New Voices 24 Hour Plays (Old Vic); The Death of Cool (Tristan Bates); Gaudeamus (Arcola); Guardians (Edinburgh Pleasance/Theatre 503); Cargo (Edinburgh Pleasance/Oval House), Doctor Faustus (Nottingham Lakeside Theatre).
As assistant director, theatre includes: Gaslight (Old Vic); A Respectable Wedding (Young Vic); As You Like It (Mountview).
Awards include: Jerwood Directors Award 2007 for the forthcoming production of dirty butterfly (Young Vic); Fringe First 2005 for Guardians.

Gregory Motton (translator)
(THE GOOD FAMILY)
For the Royal Court: Ambulance, Downfall, The Terrible Voice of Satan, The World's Biggest Diamond.
Other theatre includes: Chicken (Riverside Studios); Looking at You, Again (Leicester Haymarket); A Message for the Broken Hearted (Liverpool Playhouse); Cat and Mouse (Sheep); In Praise of Progress (Théâtre de L'Odeon, Paris); A Little Satire

(Gate); A Monologue (Musée Daupinois, Grenoble); God's Island (Théâtre de la Tempête, Paris); Gengis Among the Pygmies (La Comédie Française, Paris).
Translations include: Miss Julie, The Father, Creditors, The Comrades, The Burned Site, The Ghost Sonata, The Storm, The Pelican, The Black Glove, The Great Highway, The Dance of Death I and II, Swanwhite, Easter, The Name, Nightsongs, Someone is Going to Come, Woyzeck.
Radio includes: The Jug, Lazy Brien.

Samantha Spiro
Theatre includes: Two Thousand Years, Cleo Camping Emmanuel and Dick (National); A Little Night Music (Chicago Shakespeare's Theatre); A Midsummer Night's Dream (Crucible); Bedroom Farce (Aldwych); Merrily We Roll Along (Donmar); As You Like It (Crucible/Lyric); Jumpers (Birmingham Rep); Roots (Watford Palace/Oxford); As You Like It (West Yorkshire Playhouse/Bristol); Teechers (Hull Truck/No. I tour); On the Piste (Hull Truck); How the Other Half Loves (Theatre Royal, Windsor); Glyn & 'It' (Yvonne Arnaud/tour); A Midsummer Night's Dream (London/Middle East); Tons of Money (Mercury, Colchester); A Midsummer Night's Dream, As you Like It, Lady Be Good, Macbeth, The Boys from Syracuse (Regent's Park Open Air).
Television includes: After You've Gone, Coupling, M.I.T., Cold Feet, TV Go Home, Noble & Silver, The Bill.
Radio includes: Horst Buchholz and Other Stories, Waiting For Di, Tony's Little Sister and The Paradox of Monasticism, Otherkin, Sad Girl, Talking to Strangers, The Pipers Chair, Gospel According to Mary, Snap, Spring Forward Fall Back, Don't Step on the Cracks, Little Cinderellas, By the Coast of Coromandel, Beside the Seaside.
Film includes: Tomorrow La Scala!, From Hell, Cor Blimey, Beyond Bedlam.
Awards include: Joseph Jefferson Best Supporting Actress in a Musical Award 2004 (A Little Night Music); Olivier and Whatsonstage.com Best Actress in a Musical Awards 2001 (Merrily We Roll Along).

Jeremy Swift

For the Royal Court: Honeymoon Suite.
Other theatre includes: Abigail's Party
(Hampstead/Ambassador's); Feel Good
(Hampstead); The Slight Witch (Birmingham
Rep.); Three Sisters (Out of Joint); What the
Butler Saw, Devil's Disciple, Mother Courage,
Peer Gynt (National); A Midsummer Night's
Dream (ETT).
Television includes: Trevor Island, Live Girls,
M.I. High, 55 Degrees North, Casualty,
The Smoking Room, Reversals, Bertie &
Elizabeth, Barbara, Put Out More Fags,
The Thing About Vince, Bostock's Cup,
A Christmas Carol, The S Club, Vanity Fair,
Roger Roger, The Grand, Blind Men,
The Student Prince, Pirates, Next of Kin,
Dalziel & Pascoe, An Actor's Life for Me,
Paul Merton Show.
Film includes: Last Battle Dreamer, King Jeff,
Boy 'A', Fred Claus, Amazing Grace,
Oliver Twist, To Kill a King, Gosford Park,
Dark Blue World, Mr Love.

Ultz (designer)

For the Royal Court: The Winterling,
Stoning Mary, A Girl in a Car with a Man,
Fresh Kills, The Weather, Bear Hug, Bone,
Fallout, The Night Heron, Fireface, Lift Off,
Mojo (& Steppenwolf, Chicago).
As designer: Sixteen productions for the
RSC including Good (& Broadway), The Art
of Success (& Manhattan Theatre Club);
The Black Prince, Me and Mamie O'Rourke,
A Madhouse in Goa, Animal Crackers
(West End); Slavs! (Hampstead); Arturo Ui,
Ramayana (National); Hobson's Choice,
A Respectable Wedding (Young Vic).
Opera includes: Xerxes, La Clemenza di
Tito, The Rake's Progress (Bavarian State
Opera); The Bitter Tears of Petra Von Kant
(ENO); Macbeth (Glyndebourne).
As director and designer: Summer Holiday
(Blackpool Opera House/Apollo/UK tour/
South African tour); Jesus Christ Superstar
(Aarhus/Copenhagen); Don Giovanni,
Cosi fan tutte (in Japanese for Tokyo Globe);
A Midsummer Night's Dream (National Arts
Centre, Ottawa); The Blacks (co-directed,
Market Theatre, Johannesburg/Stadsteater,
Stockholm); The Screens (California);
The Maids, Deathwatch (co-directed RSC);

Perikles (Stadsteater, Stockholm); Snowbull
(Hampstead); The Public, The Taming of the
Shrew, Pericles, Baiju Bawra, Da Boyz,
The Blacks Remixed (co-directed with DJ
Excalibah), Pied Piper – A Hip Hop Dance
Revolution (as Associate Artist at Theatre
Royal Stratford East).
Awards include: Olivier Award for
Outstanding Achievement in an Affiliated
Theatre 2007 for Pied Piper – A Hip Hop
Dance Revolution.

Trevor Wallace (lighting designer)

For the Royal Court: Notes on Falling
Leaves, Bone, Fresh Kills, A Day in Dull
Armour.
Theatre includes: The Wild Party, Cabaret,
Sweet Charity (Electric, Guildford); The Beau
Defeated (Bellairs Playhouse, Guildford);
West Side Story (Courtyard, Stratford Upon
Avon); Marat/Sade, Dark of the Moon
(Jermyn Street); The Estate, The Gods are
not to Blame (Tiata Fahodzi); Golden Boy,
Nobody's Perfect, Kit and the Widow –
The Fat Lady Sings, Peter Pan and Snow
White (Yvonne Arnaud, Guildford); The Weir
(Theatro Technis); The Shape of Things, Bash
(Bridewell); Closer (Barn); Into the Woods,
The Changeling (Sandpit, St Albans);
The School of Night (Shattered
Windscreen); Comedy of Errors, Grimm
Tales, Richard III, Cyrano de Bergerac,
Les Enfants du Paradis, The Three
Musketeers, A Midsummer Night's Dream
(Minack, Cornwall).
Film includes: Director of Photography on
The Best Man.

THE ENGLISH STAGE COMPANY AT THE ROYAL COURT

'For me the theatre is really a religion or way of life. You must decide what you feel the world is about and what you want to say about it, so that everything in the theatre you work in is saying the same thing ... A theatre must have a recognisable attitude. It will have one, whether you like it or not.'

George Devine, first artistic director of the English Stage Company: notes for an unwritten book.

The Royal Court Theatre in London's Sloane Square has presented some of the most influential plays in modern theatre history. At the turn of the twentieth century, the Royal Court was under the direction of Harley Granville-Barker and staged plays by Ibsen, Galsworthy, Yeats, Maeterlinck and Shaw. In 1956 George Devine became the first Artistic Director of the English Stage Company at the Royal Court. His intention was to create an international theatre of experiment that was devoted to the discovery of the future in playwriting. The production of John Osborne's Look Back in Anger in 1956 ushered in a new generation of playwrights, directors, actors and designers who together established the Court as the first theatre in London that prioritised the work of contemporary playwrights. Among them were Arnold Wesker, Ann Jellicoe, Edward Bond, John Arden, Christopher Hampton and David Storey. New plays were programmed alongside classics, and the company was from its earliest days committed to producing the best new international plays, including those of Ionesco, Genet and Beckett.

In 1969 the Royal Court opened the first second space in a British theatre; the Jerwood Theatre Upstairs has been a site for radical experimentation and has introduced audiences to some of the most influential new voices of the last 40 years, including Wole Soyinka, Caryl Churchill, David Hare, Howard Brenton, Howard Barker, Peter Gill, Martin Crimp, Sam Shepard and Jim Cartwright. Many outstanding young playwrights have established their careers here; among them Joe Penhall, Sarah Kane, Roy Williams, Rebecca Prichard, Mark Ravenhill, Martin McDonagh, Conor McPherson, Simon Stephens and debbie tucker green.

The Royal Court's Artistic Programme is only partially about the work seen on its stages. Many of its resources, and indeed the roots of the organisation, are devoted to the discovery and nurturing of new writers and the development of new plays. The Royal Court is in the business of asking questions about the world we live in and about what a play itself can be. The theatre's aim is to support both new and established writers in exploring new territory.

The Royal Court has a rich and productive infrastructure for the discovery and development of playwrights:

photo: Stephen Cummiiskey

International Programme
Since 1992 the Royal Court has initiated and developed lasting relationships with international playwrights and theatre practitioners. Creative dialogue is ongoing with theatre practitioners from many countries, including Brazil, Cuba, France, Germany, India, Mexico, Nigeria, Palestine, Russia, Spain and Syria. Many of the world's most promising and exciting playwrights have presented their plays on the stages of the Royal Court, among them Marcos Barbosa, Roland Schimmelpfennig, Marius von Mayenburg, Vassily Sigarev, the Presnyakov brothers and David Gieselmann. All of these influential projects are generously supported by the Genesis Foundation and the British Council.

The Young Writers Programme
The Young Writers Programme seeks to open up theatre to the most exciting and diverse range of new voices around today, encouraging and inspiring young writers to use theatre as a means of exploring their world, and helping them to flourish as artists. Week-long intensive playwriting projects for the 13-16 and 16-19 age groups are run during school holidays and each season playwriting groups for the 18-25 age group are led by resident playwriting tutor Leo Butler.

Rough Cuts
The Royal Court's plays have frequently challenged the artistic, social and political orthodoxy of the day, pushing back the boundaries of what is acceptable or possible. That tradition of experiment and provocation is intensified in the Rough Cuts seasons of experimental collaborations between playwrights and other artists, which are presented as raw and immediate works-in-progress in the Jerwood Theatre Upstairs.

The Royal Court's long and successful history of innovation has been built by generations of gifted and imaginative individuals. For information on the many exciting ways you can help support the theatre, please contact the Development Department on 020 7565 5079.

INTERNATIONAL PLAYWRIGHTS AT THE ROYAL COURT

Since 1992 the Royal Court has placed a renewed emphasis on the development of international work and a creative dialogue now exists with theatre practitioners all over the world including Brazil, Cuba, France, Germany, India, Mexico, Nigeria, Palestine, Romania, Russia, Spain and Syria, and with writers from seven countries from the Near East and North Africa region. All of these development projects are supported by either the British Council or the Genesis Foundation.

The Royal Court has produced new International plays through this programme since 1997. Recent work includes On Insomnia and Midnight by Edgar Chías (Mexico), My Name is Rachel Corrie, Amid the Clouds by Amir Reza Koohestani (Iran), Way to Heaven by Juan Mayorga (Spain), At the Table and Almost Nothing by Marcos Barbosa (Brazil), Plasticine, Black Milk and Ladybird by Vassily Sigarev (Russia), Terrorism by the Presnyakov Brothers (Russia), The Ugly One by Marius von Mayenburg (Germany), Kebab by Gianina Carbunariu (Romania) and Free Outgoing by Anupama Chandrasekhar (India). All of these productions have been supported by the Genesis Foundation.

The Good Family was first performed as a rehearsed reading at the Royal Court as part of the New Plays from the Nordic Countries in December 2002. Natalia Vorozhbit attended the International Residency in 2005 and has been involved with the Royal Court's work in Moscow since 1999. The Khomenko Family Chronicles was first performed as a rehearsed reading, as part of Small Talk: Big Picture at the Royal Court in November 2006.

The Good Family and The Khomenko Family Chronicles are presented as part of International Playwrights, A Genesis Project, produced by the Royal Court's International Department:

Associate Director **Elyse Dodgson**
International Administrator **Chris James**
International Assistant **William Drew**

The Genesis Foundation supports the Royal Court's International Playwrights Programme. To find and develop the next generation of professional playwrights, Genesis funds workshops in diverse countries as well as residencies at the Royal Court. The Foundation's involvement extends to productions and rehearsed readings. Genesis helps the Royal Court offer a springboard for young writers to greater public and critical attention. For more information, please visit www.genesisfoundation.org.uk

PROGRAMME SUPPORTERS

The Royal Court (English Stage Company Ltd) receives its principal funding from Arts Council England, London. It is also supported financially by a wide range of private companies, charitable and public bodies, and earns the remainder of its income from the box office and its own trading activities.

The Genesis Foundation supports the Royal Court's work with International Playwrights.

The Jerwood Charity supports new plays by new playwrights through the Jerwood New Playwrights series.

The Artistic Director's Chair is supported by a lead grant from The Peter Jay Sharp Foundation, contributing to the activities of the Artistic Director's office. Over the past ten years the BBC has supported the Gerald Chapman Fund for directors.

American Friends of the Royal Court are primarily focused on raising funds to enable the theatre to produce new work by emerging American writers. AFRCT has also supported the participation of young artists in the Royal Court's acclaimed International Residency. Contact: 001-212-946-5724.

UK premiere
17 January – 1 March 2008

the vertical hour

by David Hare

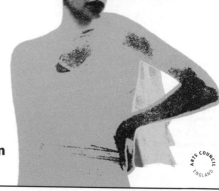

Cast includes **Indira Varma**
(*Rome* for the BBC and
The Vortex for the Donmar)

Tickets £10, £15, £25
www.royalcourttheatre.com
020 7565 5000

Joakim Pirinen
THE GOOD FAMILY
TRANSLATED BY GREGORY MOTTON

and

Natalia Vorozhbit
THE KHOMENKO FAMILY CHRONICLES
TRANSLATED BY SASHA DUGDALE

OBERON BOOKS
LONDON

First published in 2007 by Oberon Books Ltd
521 Caledonian Road, London N7 9RH
Tel: 020 7607 3637 / Fax: 020 7607 3629
email: info@oberonbooks.com
www.oberonbooks.com

A catalogue record for this book is available from the British Library.

Cover illustration by Ida Swarczewskaja

ISBN: 978-1-84002-808-9

Printed in Great Britain by Antony Rowe Ltd, Chippenham.

Contents

THE GOOD FAMILY

Characters

LASSE

JANNE

LENA

EVA

SCENE 1

An evening in June. The thrush is singing and the heads of the flowers are heavy with sleep. In the garden of the family's detached house there are a set of garden chairs and a suite of garden furniture of wood-effect plastic. The cushions are still in the seats. The day has been warm and there is still time left before the dew falls. LASSE and JANNE stroll about the edge of the lawn and breathe in the scent of the earth. Behind them, two french windows open into the living room.

LASSE: The weather is really lovely this evening, Janne.

JANNE: Yes, Dad. The sky is completely cloudless.

LASSE: It's glorious out this time of year.

JANNE: Just the right temperature too.

LASSE: And we're going to have just as good weather tomorrow. Did your exam go alright today, by the way?

JANNE: Oh yes, extremely well. Everyone passed! I had loads of stamina and jumped higher, longer and quicker than ever! The teacher praised me extra much, and I got top marks in everything. So did everyone actually.

LASSE: That's really nice to hear. Congratulations Janne!

JANNE: (*Picks up a closed box that is lying on the lawn and carries it with one arm to the door, beside which he places it on the ground.*) Look, I can hold the box with one arm!

LASSE: You're as strong as a superman. I'm your friend aren't I, Janne, I hope?

JANNE: One hundred per cent, Dad. Have you had a good day too?

LASSE: Yes, you could say. It is rather a privilege to have the whole world as a workplace, and it's going very well for my company. The prognoses have been very good and we are on a steadily upward curve, but today our profits beat all records. And besides I managed to arrange a big foreign order for the company during a coffee break, so now we can take on a bigger workforce. That's good for employment, and our finance director said it means a decent salary rise for all our employees for that matter.

JANNE: That's great Dad!

LASSE: Thanks Janne. Look, here comes our Lena.

LENA: (*From the lawn.*) Hello Dad, hello Janne!

JANNE: Hello Lena, you're just in time for dinner.

LASSE: Your hair is nice Lena.

LENA: (*Lets her father feel her hair.*) Thanks Dad. It's a new perm and blow wave. I slept over at Pelle's last night, he helped me with my homework.

LASSE: He's a good boy is Pelle.

LENA: Oh yes! And then I helped him, we really work well together Pelle and me.

JANNE: It's fun having my best friend and my sister going out together. Oh Lena, Ulla rang. She asked me to say that it would be nice if you could phone her when you have the time. You can ring whenever you like she said.

LENA: Sweet of you Janne, I will. What fun it will be to talk to her!

JANNE: (*Goes through the living room door.*) Say hello to her for me. I'll go in and help Mum lay the table.

LASSE: That's kind of you Janne.

LENA: Dad I think Janne is rather keen on Ulla.

LASSE: Yes he seems particularly in love today.

LENA: (*She does the splits.*) See how lissom I am now!

LASSE: (*Applauds.*) Phenomenal Lena! You're a fully fledged ballerina.

LENA: (*Up out of the splits.*) Thanks Dad. I'm going to keep practising until I'm perfect.

LASSE: (*Hugs his daughter from behind.*) And everything is well between you and Pelle?

LENA: Yes, Pelle is so sweet. I can talk to him about everything. We have such fun together, we just laugh all the time. I love him. And we have a great time in bed too.

LASSE: That sounds nice. I think it's important to be able to get on well together, sexually too. Like Eva and I.

LENA: We have a super cosy time my Pelle and me.

LASSE: (*Leaves the embrace and turns his attention to the grass.*) Have you seen how luscious the lawn is?

LENA: Yes, it's completely smooth. You're a really good gardener Dad. Green is a colour I love.

LASSE: Have you seen how many daisies we have? I think daisies must be my favourite flower.

LENA: Daisies are the most beautiful flower I know.

EVA: (*Calls to her husband from inside.*) Dinner's ready.

LASSE: (*Picks a rose from the climber by the doorpost.*) I wonder what's for dinner today.

LASSE and LENA go inside.

SCENE 2

When LASSE and LENA come into the kitchen, EVA and JANNE stand by the table, which has been set for a meal. There are four plates with cutlery and glasses, butter, coarse bread in slices together with crisp bread in a basket, potatoes in a saucepan, salad in a bowl, a dish of brown sauce, skimmed milk and iced water in jugs, and not least a fine roast joint. The saucepans and serving dishes, which are hot, have been placed upon homemade mats to preserve the tablecloth. Perhaps on each plate there are monogrammed serviettes in holders. Half of the joint is carved into slices.

LENA: Hello Mum.

EVA: Hello my little kitten.

LASSE: A right royal roast! Have you ever seen the like. For that I want to give the lady chef a red rose.

EVA: My flower king! Thank you. A red rose. Red is the most beautiful colour I know. You are a real honeybear. I'll put this rose in a vase on the table so we can all enjoy it.

EVA puts the vase in the centre of the table. They serve themselves food and each passes the dishes around clockwise to their neighbour.

LASSE: (*Lifts up a saucepan and lights upon the homemade coaster beneath it.*) These coasters you have made are really elegant and durable Janne, a real showpiece.

JANNE: I'm glad you like them Dad, the main thing is that they protect the table, if they are decorative at the same time then that is an extra bonus.

EVA: Take enough now all of you so that you get full my sweetie-pies.

JANNE: Mmm, the potatoes are extraordinarily well cooked.

LASSE: Splendid potatoes, and the roast is really grand! If the king got a taste of your roast Eva, he'd know why it's called a right royal steak.

EVA: Lasse, you are my king.

JANNE: The meat is scrumptious Mum, you really know the art of seasoning a meal.

EVA: (*Offers the salad bowl.*) Take some salad if you like.

JANNE: Iceberg lettuce! Delicious! Tasty and good for you!

LASSE: The sauce is choice. And what an appetising golden brown colour it has.

EVA: Apropos colour, it really has become even more homely and cosy here in the kitchen since you repainted it, my little artists.

LASSE: It was a quick job too, thanks to Janne.

JANNE: The new acrylic paints are so quick-drying and easy to work with.

LENA: Yellow is a colour that makes you happy.

LASSE: Especially this shade of yellow, you chose exactly right girls.

EVA: Just think! We chose exactly the same colour, Lena. And Janne helped me get the colour of the sauce.

LASSE: This sauce is an absolute delicacy. You know just how to season a dish – you're so good at cooking.

LENA: Yes the sauce is yummy Janne.

JANNE: A bit of butter and flour in the meat's juices, herbs and spices. Simple.

LASSE: Is there bread and butter too! I think I'll have a slice.

EVA: Yes, do sweetheart, it's brand new health-bread, really cheap and with extra B-vitamins. I'd be so happy if you'd taste it, my connoisseur.

JANNE: I read this article this morning –

LASSE: (*Drops his bread on the floor.*) Whoops, I seem to have dropped my bread and butter on the floor.

LENA: (*Picks up the fallen slice.*) Lucky! You dropped it butter-side up.

EVA: I'll make you a new one.

LASSE: Thank you dearest. You were going to tell us something Janne.

JANNE: That's alright Dad. Oh yeah, I read an article today, very well written. In essence it said that you gain in the long run if you eat nourishing bread with B-vitamins.

EVA: That sounds like good common sense I think. Bread is so nice, and you feel even better if you eat well.

JANNE: (*Lifts a glass of milk.*) One ought to drink nourishing things too. Milk gives the required amount of energy.

LENA: May I have some more Mum? It so nice!

EVA: I'm so glad you like the food, my angel.

JANNE: Can I make dinner tomorrow Mum?

LENA: And me the day after?

EVA: Of course you can darlings. And on Friday we are all four invited to Hasse and Greta's for dinner.

JANNE: Oo, it's always so cosy there...

LENA: Hasse and Greta are really sweet.

EVA: They're popping over later tonight actually.

LASSE: How nice! We always have so much to talk about together. It's so nice to have friends. Maybe we can plan our holiday with them tonight?

EVA: Yes I'm sure we can, and I have got in some spare ribs for our lovely neighbours.

LASSE: Wonderful! Spare ribs are the tops!

JANNE: Thank you for dinner Mum darling.

LENA: Thank you for dinner Mum. You always make such wonderful food. It was super!

LASSE: The food was superb Eva.

EVA: Thank you my sunshine saints.

LASSE: Right, now today marks a unique and special event.

JANNE / LASSE / EVA: (*They stand up and burst out in unison.*) It's our Lena's birthday! Happy eighteenth birthday dear darling Lena! (*Sing.*) Happy birthday to you, happy birthday to you, happy birthday dear Lena, happy birthday to you!

LASSE: Three big cheers for Lena. Hipp hipp –

JANNE / LASSE / EVA: Hurrah!

LASSE: Hipp hipp –

JANNE / LASSE / EVA: Hurrah!

LASSE: Hipp hipp –

JANNE / LASSE / EVA: Hurrah!

LENA: How kind. Thank you. You sung so nicely. This morning Pelle gave me coffee in bed and now I'm getting even more birthday celebrations.

EVA: (*Passes a gift-wrapped parcel to LENA.*) Happy birthday, apple of my eye!

LENA: A present? For me? You are so wonderful. What lovely wrapping paper. Ooooh, what a lovely long-sleeved jumper! Red and blue, my favourite colours. Thank you, thank you, you're so kind. I must try it on at once! (*Exit.*)

JANNE: Mum, can I take care of the dishes today?

EVA: Of course Janne, if you want to, sweet boy!

JANNE: I like washing-up. It's so relaxing to work with your hands in warm water and the new environmentally friendly washing-up liquid is gentle on your skin, and then I think it gives you such a wonderful sense of satisfaction to see the draining board clean and everything in its place.

EVA: It's so good that you want to wash up, my hero. Now I can use the time for something else useful.

LENA: (*Enter dressed in the new birthday jumper.*) It fits perfectly! Such quality! Thank you, you're so kind!

EVA: (*Takes out an envelope.*) Both sets of grandparents have sent a card as well. To our little angel, it says on the envelope.

LENA: (*Takes it, opens it and takes out a card.*) What a beautiful card. So many presents. Warm congratulations on your special day, our dear darling little grandchild, from grandma and grandpa, and grandma and grandpa, it says. So sweet of them! What stylish handwriting!

JANNE: (*He too passes a parcel to LENA.*) Happy birthday little sister.

LENA: Janne, have you bought me a present too? What lovely wrapping paper, I'll open it at once. Oooh such a lovely short-sleeved jumper! Black and white are among the best colours I know. I'll try it on at last. (*Exit.*)

EVA: So thoughtful of you to buy a present as well Janne. It was a surprise for me too.

JANNE: Of course little sister must have a present.

LASSE: I wonder if Lena would like to do something special tonight seeing as it's her birthday.

EVA: On your birthday we played dice, that was fun and pleasant.

JANNE: Yes it was great fun. Dice is exciting, everyone can win.

LASSE: Let's ask Lena.

LENA: (*Enters.*) It fits perfectly. What quality!

EVA: My little fashion queen. It's fabulously stylish.

LASSE: Really stunning!

LENA: (*Hugs JANNE.*) Thank you big brother. I'm going to wear this a lot. Mum, please can I do the washing-up tonight, it's so nice to have your hands in hot water and the washing-up liquid is so gentle.

JANNE: Whoops, I've already offered to do the washing-up. I did it when you were out trying on the jumper.

LENA: We can help each other, one washes one dries.

JANNE: Ace, let's! That way we get company too.

EVA: I know exactly what I'm going to do while you do the washing-up. I'm going to hang the washing.

LASSE: Before we get started with our tasks, I'd like to ask
   Lena if there is anything in particular she would like to do
   on her birthday.

LENA: Couldn't we play dice? It's such fun!

LASSE: A brilliant idea, Lena. I think we ought to do that.

JANNE: I'll fetch the games board from the toy cupboard.

EVA: And I'll put on the kettle for some herb tea so we can
   quench our thirsts after the game.

   Exit.

SCENE 3

*LASSE and LENA carry out the plates to the kitchen. When that is done
they go out to the living room where JANNE has returned with a small
card table of a height to allow players to stand around it. EVA returns
from the kitchen and they all gather round the playing surface. They stand
around the table clockwise: LENA, EVA, LASSE and JANNE. LASSE has
taken out four dice and a small pad and pencil.*

LASSE: I suggest we each have our own dice; we all throw
   once per turn and the winner of each turn is the one who
   throws the highest. I'll keep score.

JANNE: That's good and fair.

EVA: I think the birthday girl should start, if she wants.

LENA: That's nice. This is going to be great fun, here we go.
   I'm throwing the dice. A six, first go! Yippie!

LASSE: What a lucky throw!

EVA: My little four-leafed clover.

JANNE: Well done Lena!

EVA: My turn. One.

LENA: There'll be other goes, Mum.

JANNE: Hold on now. One for me too.

LASSE: Now it's my go. Look at that. I got a one as well; six, one, one, one. You won this turn, Lena, easily.

LENA: Imagine that! I won on my birthday! First go too! Now it's your turn to start, Mum.

EVA: Oh how exciting! One, two, three, go! A six! What a fluke.

JANNE: Good throw, Mum!

LASSE: A great shot.

LENA: Bravo, Mum!

LASSE: Here I go, one.

JANNE: One here as well.

LENA: One for me too. Six, one, one, one. You won this time, Mum!

JANNE: Nice work, Mum.

EVA: Oh what fun, little me carried off the victory.

LASSE: Now I'll start. Easy does it, here comes the dice, a one.

JANNE: There'll be other chances, Dad. Look, I threw a six! The highest possible. Pure luck!

LENA: Good throw, Janne. I got a one.

EVA: Oh it's exciting now. Here's the dice. One.

LASSE: One, six, one, and the first prize goes, as clear as day, to Janne. Well deserved too, I think.

EVA: And it's your turn to start too, my gambling king.

JANNE: It's great to win. The dice rolls, and gives a three. Three for me. Your turn Lena.

LENA: I'm shaking it, rolling it, and it's a two. Come on now, Mum, it's your turn to show us what you can do.

EVA: I'm shaking it, I'm throwing it, oh dear! The dice has bounced onto the floor.

LASSE: Of course you must have another turn, but you can keep the score you got if you prefer it, it's perfectly alright whichever, I think.

Agreement from JANNE and LENA.

EVA: I think I'll chose to throw again. It's like getting an extra turn and then it's more exciting too, I think.

JANNE: (*Fetches his mother's dice from the floor and hands it to her.*) A new, fresh turn, Mum here's your dice.

EVA: Thank you my pigeon. I'd better give it a proper shake, throw carefully and hoopla! It's a one.

LASSE: Duck boys! Here comes another, and it's a four. Now let's count up. Three, two, one, four.

EVA: Then you've won Lasse, my lucky mascot.

LASSE: Fancy that! But it evened out in the end.

JANNE: But you carried off the last round, absolutely.

LENA: Congratulations, Dad.

EVA: I think the tea's ready now, my little dice-playing companions.

SCENE 4

JANNE and LENA seat themselves in a three-seater sofa. LASSE sits down in an adjacent armchair. A coffee table stands in front of the sofa.

LASSE: It's going to be really nice to have a cup of tea.

JANNE: The new dice are lovely to play with, just the right size and perfectly rounded so that they roll just right.

LENA: Like my new bicycle! It rolls completely friction-free especially on all the downhill slopes, and the brakes work the moment you apply them. Grey is such a good colour. Both exclusive and discrete. It's a really first-rate bicycle.

EVA: (*Comes in with a tray on which stand four teacups and a teapot.*) Here you are, I hope the tea tastes good, there are seven different herbs included, according to the declaration of contents on the packet.

JANNE: Talking of which, Mum I wanted to thank you for the new herb shampoo you gave me. It really keeps my hair in trim and it smells good too.

EVA: Your hair is really light and vigorous looking, my dream prince.

LASSE: (*He has poured his cup and tasted it.*) What fantastic tea! What an aroma! You really see summer meadows before you! Tea really is an incomparable drink, isn't it? It gives you clarity, somehow.

LENA: Yes, tea both perks you up and quenches your thirst and warms you, all at the same time.

EVA: (*Secretively.*) Hehehe.

JANNE: What are you giggling about, Mum?

EVA: Sorry, when Lena said warm, I thought of Christmas Eve, and that made me think of a joke I heard today.

LENA: Oh Mum, do tell us.

EVA: Shall I really?

LASSE / JANNE: Yes!

EVA: Well, once you've said A you might as well say B. It was Mrs Andreason who told me, she's always so witty. It goes like this. Little Emma, five years old, is standing in the hall when her father comes in with a big Christmas tree. It's the day before Christmas Eve. He carries the tree into the living room, where there is a Christmas-tree-stand, already set up. Emma's father sets the base of the tree in the stand and screws it down into it so that it stands straight and firm. Emma watches all this wide-eyed. What shall we do now? Emma asks her father. We're going to decorate the Christmas tree, said Emma's father to Emma, but then Emma runs away. After a long time she comes back. And now it's Emma's father's turn to be surprised. Little Emma, you see, has brought with her some paint brushes and a tin of paint from Daddy's shed. What are you going to do with all that? asks her father, and Emma answers… Do you know what she answers?

LASSE / JANNE / LENA: (*In unison and in expectation.*) No?

EVA: I'm going to decorate the Christmas tree.

All laugh long and heartily.

LENA: What a sweet little story!

LASSE: Yes, the word decorate can indeed mean both painting or wall-papering, and to hang decorations on a tree!

JANNE: That's exactly the kind of funny thing children do say. Thanks for the tea and the joke, Mum. I'll tell that one to my friends. Would you like to do the washing-up with me now, Lena?

LENA: Oh yes, I certainly would. Washing-up here I come! Thanks for the tea, Mum.

EVA: Thanks yourselves my little sugar lumps.

JANNE and LENA go out.

What a helpful family I've got. I find it so liberating that we all help out around the house.

LASSE: Working together is always enriching in my experience

EVA: That's exactly what I find in my new job, we work together both intimately and effectively. My colleagues are quite fantastic people, my office is so well designed and the decoration of the office space is really something to feast your eyes upon. We have such a nice time in the breaks, and the work we have to do is so varied. It's uplifting that leisure-time and working hours can compliment each other. Every day brings new challenges. Do you know, it's as if mathematical questions were to contain their own answers, everything goes so smoothly, it really is uplifting. How stimulating it is to be able to be creative!

LASSE: Eva, I get quite excited when I hear that you are getting along so well.

EVA: Yes, I feel as if I'm developing as a person all the time, just from having a positive job that I get along with. The washing facilities for the staff are well adapted too.

LASSE: How nice it is that society offers so many different types of work at the same time as people have such different interests and abilities.

EVA: The freedom to shape your own life is very important, I think.

LASSE: That's exactly what was described so vividly in the book you gave me.

EVA: My little reading companion, did you like it?

LASSE: Did I? It's a marvellous novel. A virtuoso composition, stylistically brilliant, and fun at the same time. The train of thought in the book is crystal clear, like spring water, very entertaining.

EVA: I enjoyed it immensely when I read it. It gives you so much when you can understand culture that you enjoy.

LASSE: The chapter when the princes relax in the shade of the palm trees below the silver palace was very strong indeed. They had just discovered that enchanted gold. The butterflies were competing with the hummingbirds around the orchids, the rabbits were playing amongst the wild strawberries down the slope. Suddenly a maiden glides through the sunshiney haze. She knows exactly what the princes want. She offers them watermelons and grapefruits. It was so engagingly written, it was almost as if I was there myself.

EVA: You're so sensitive, my velvet star.

LASSE: And they said such wise things. For example that you should be able to live richly on your income at the same time as taxes should be enough to cover society's needs.

EVA: Yes, it's just before they travel out into space. Lasse, it has suddenly struck me that society is one whole, made up of variations, like a symphony.

LASSE: That's very poetic. You're so intelligent!

EVA: (*Strokes his cheek.*) Thank you, my little sweetie-pie. But you are the real bard.

LASSE: I'm going to write out my poems tonight so that my publisher has them tomorrow.

EVA: And I'm going to finish my play. May I read your lyric poems when I'm finished?

LASSE: Of course you can. May I read your drama?

EVA: Of course, my dear, beloved teddy-bear. But first I must hang up the washing.

LASSE: Then I'll help you.

EVA: My little helper.

LASSE: I love you Eva.

EVA: Oh Lasse I love you too.

LASSE: Eva, together you and I create our love. It's born to be constantly renewed and deepened. Love is strengthened every second throughout eternity, and through the inner tenderness of faithfulness and friendship.

EVA: Love is the finest thing that can exist between two people.

LASSE: I love you just as much this evening as the day we married and still my love for you continues to grow all the time, can you understand that?

EVA: Yes, I can understand!

LASSE: How beautiful you are, Eva.

EVA: Oh mon cheri, so you say.

LASSE: I really mean it. You just get more beautiful every day.

EVA: Oh my nicey! You always say such wonderful sweet things

LASSE: You're a very attractive woman, Eva.

EVA: And you are every bit a man.

JANNE: (*Comes in.*) Er, Mum, Dad.

EVA: Have you finished the washing-up already? Goodness me!

JANNE: With Lena as a workmate, it's done in a flash.

LASSE: Ten minutes. That was very gallant of you! You're a couple of professionals.

JANNE: Er, Mum and Dad, there's something I'd like to talk to you about.

EVA: Come and sit in the sofa darling.

JANNE: Yes, thanks. Gosh the tea is still warm and there's plenty left. Our new teapot is fantastic.

EVA: You can talk to us about anything, Janne.

JANNE: Of course Mum. There was just one thing I'd better tell you. I'm a homosexual.

EVA: My little ray of sunshine!

LASSE: That's great Janne! It's really fantastic that you can say openly that you're a homosexual.

EVA: My beloved son. I feel as if you have shown wonderful faith in us to share this confidence with us.

LASSE: And Janne, it's really super that you've already realised that you are homosexual. It must give you a liberating sense of reassurance, I expect.

JANNE: Yes, I've already met a boy. He's called Olle. He's homosexual too. It was love at first sight. We fell head over heels in love straight away. It just clicked and now we are together.

EVA: That's just how it was with Lasse and I.

JANNE: Olle is a really lovely boy. We can talk to each other about everything, and he's got a marvellous sense of humour. Oh my heart throbs when I think of Olle!

EVA: I'm sure you and Olle are going to love each other just as much as Lasse and I love each other.

LASSE: Love is the best thing there is. We were just talking about it. Oh, the phone's ringing. I'll get it. (*Exit.*)

JANNE: You must meet Olle. He's so pretty. He's got a very muscular body and his hair is like burnished gold.

EVA: Do you think Olle would like to come here for dinner with us, some time that suits you both?

JANNE: Absolutely. Olle has said that he's really looking forward to meeting you and Dad. Any day is fine.

EVA: Then I'll prepare a really tasty meal. What do you say to fish?

JANNE: It's Olle's favourite food!

LENA enters.

EVA: Hello my sweetheart.

JANNE: My boyfriend is coming to dinner, any day now. I've just told Mum and Dad that I'm a homosexual.

LENA: (*Sits in the sofa next to JANNE and EVA.*) Wow! That's so completely cool! It sounds really exciting, I think it's lovely. I really understand that you like boys, they're so soft and cuddly.

EVA: (*With her arms around her children.*) My dear children, I just want to tell you that I love you limitlessly. I want you to know that we're always here, Dad and I. We're ready to help you with everything and you can talk to us about absolutely everything. We'll always be with you. We're always going to have a lovely time together.

LENA: Darling Mum.

JANNE: Thanks Mum. It felt good to tell you about my love for Olle. Oh how I love you all!

LENA: What fun. Now you and I can talk about boys together Janne!

LASSE: (*Enters.*) It was Hans and Greta on the phone. They're going to drop in tomorrow evening instead, and that's even better I think, because then I'll have time to finish all my work this evening.

EVA: So can I. Then maybe we can drive down to the beach tomorrow?

LENA: Oh yes let's. We can take a packed lunch and have a picnic.

LASSE: What a radiant idea, to go sunbathing.

EVA: Then I'll pack some towels and swimming costumes this evening so that we can leave whenever we want tomorrow morning. But first I'll hang up the washing.

LENA: No, you don't need to. And do you know why? Because I've already done it. I took the opportunity when we'd finished doing the washing-up. The washing was lovely, whiter than white.

EVA: My pet, you are an angel. What would I do without you?

LENA: I'll go and phone Ulla. What fun it's going to be to talk to her! And then it's my job to make the sandwiches for our trip. I'll probably take a shower too. (*Exit.*)

JANNE: I'll go for an evening walk. I'll take the short cut down to the church, turn off by the hypermarket and cut through the path alongside the back gardens on the way home. It's just about the right distance for a walk. I'll be back soon. Have a nice time while I'm gone.

LASSE: Have a pleasant walk, Janne.

EVA: Bye-bye, my pride and joy.

Exit JANNE.

LASSE closes his eyes, takes a deep breath.

EVA: What are you thinking my philosopher?

LASSE: It suddenly occurred to me how wonderful life is. When I think over everything I've got. A beautiful and functional house, a highly paid dream-job, I have my health, and above all two clever children to be proud of and a wife to love. Let me show you what I got today. (*Takes out his wallet.*) Look, eight unlimited credit cards. The biggest is for you.

EVA: Oh thank you. My own financial genius!

LASSE: Perhaps I should do a little physical work. I'll carry in the box, then it'll be done. (*Exit.*)

EVA: (*Moves the sofa ever so slightly.*) Then I'll prepare a space for it here. Is that alright, my iron man?

LASSE: (*Enters, carrying the box with one arm.*) Easy-peasey, it weighs less than a nightingale's feather.

EVA: (*Puts the box in its place.*) How charming it is, it looks really decorative there.

LASSE: (*Returns to the garden door.*) Yes, it looks good there, alright! That's that sorted out!

EVA: (*Goes to her husband's side in the doorway.*) What a resplendent garden we have, anyway! What sweet perfumes! It makes you quite drunk and blissful with delirium. And to think that it's still light outside!

LASSE: What luxuriant greenery. The hawthorn is blooming pink and the lilacs are purple, the peonies are glowing red and the cherry blossom compete in whiteness with the bird cherry.

EVA: And it's been a perfect day too.

LASSE: This summer seems eternal.

EVA: It feels so nice that it's always going to be like this.

LASSE and EVA kiss and go inside the house.

Curtain.

THE KHOMENKO FAMILY CHRONICLES

Characters

LYOSHA KHOMENKO
Aged 9

PAPA
Lyuda Khomenko, Lyosha's mother

MAMA
Kostya Khomenko, Lyosha's father

A hospital ward. LYOSHA, a pale little boy, is lying in bed. His father and pregnant mother are sitting by the bed. His mother is fussing over the blankets.

MAMA: Does it hurt here, Lyosha?

LYOSHA: Yes.

MAMA: And here?

LYOSHA: (*Considering.*) Yes.

PAPA: Stop behaving like some girl – hurts here, hurts there. You're a man. Learn to put up with the pain.

MAMA looks angrily at PAPA.

MAMA: You put up with it, why don't you.

PAPA: Don't shout in front of the boy.

MAMA: Lyosha, would you like me to call the nurse and ask her to give you another injection? To take the pain away?

LYOSHA: No, don't. I've got a sore bum from all the injections.

MAMA: (*Sobbing.*) My baby…

LYOSHA: I'm not a baby.

PAPA: He's not a baby, Lyuda. You're humiliating him.

MAMA pulls herself together. She produces some plastic bags and empties them out.

MAMA: I've brought you some pomegranate drink, love. Be sure and drink it. And here's some chicken soup. It's very good for you.

LYOSHA: It's got bits of onion in it again.

MAMA: Where? That's not onion, it's potato.

LYOSHA: Do you think I'm blind or something? Look there it is. Do you want me to be sick?

MAMA opens the soup and tries to extract the floating bits of onion with a spoon. LYOSHA watches her with disgust.

Mum, the onion's all fallen apart. I'm not going to eat it.

PAPA: Eat your chicken soup and you'll grow up big and strong.

LYOSHA: You eat it then. I'm not going to.

PAPA: Is that any way to talk to me?

LYOSHA: Yeah. What you going to do? Send me to my room?

PAPA: (*Distractedly.*) Just you wait till you get home – I'll show you what a sore bum is.

LYOSHA: Well I won't come home then.

PAPA: And where are you going to go? Until you're eighteen you don't have a choice.

LYOSHA: Yeah? And what about if I die here?

PAPA: Well. Well, I suppose. Yes. You've beaten me there.

LYOSHA is triumphant.

MAMA: Lyosha… Daddy's joking. (*To her husband.*) Think before opening your big mouth. Here. Eat this.

She gives her husband the jar of chicken soup and a spoon.

LYOSHA: Give Dad the beer instead. He could do with it.

PAPA eats the soup. He scoops up a piece of boiled onion with his spoon and eats it. LYOSHA watches with revulsion. He gags and, caught unawares, he pukes up all over the sheets.

MAMA: Oh my God, Lyosha!

PAPA stops eating the soup. He pushes it away in disgust.

PAPA: Nice one.

MAMA takes off the sheets and wipes LYOSHA with a tissue.

LYOSHA: I didn't mean to.

MAMA: It's alright.

LYOSHA: Don't ever put onion in the...

As he says 'onion' he is sick again. MAMA holds a bag out to catch it.

MAMA: I won't put any more onion in...

LYOSHA: Mam, stop saying that word...

PAPA: That's right – you give in to him. He'll grow up a selfish loser.

MAMA: Take after his dad then.

PAPA: I hope to God he does take after me.

MAMA: Have a good look in the mirror and take that back.

PAPA: Who do you want to take after then, son? Her? Or your father?

LYOSHA: I take after Grandma. Is that okay?

PAPA: (*To MAMA.*) Is this your doing?

MAMA gets out a bottle of beer for PAPA.

MAMA: I give in.

PAPA: Spoiling everyone's mood like that.

PAPA opens the beer. He drinks the whole bottle – fast, but efficiently.

My wife's one in a million. And my son's a genius.

They all relax.

PAPA: (*All matey.*) Well then, son, which of your friends came down to see you today?

LYOSHA: Natasha did.

PAPA: (*Winking meaningfully at his wife.*) Natasha.

MAMA: (*Smiling.*) Nice girl. When I think how much happiness there is in store for you two…

PAPA: Have you kissed her?

LYOSHA: Da-ad!

PAPA: Don't hang around. Get in first.

LYOSHA: Did you get in first with Mum?

PAPA: (*Unhesitatingly.*) 'Course.

MAMA coughs.

LYOSHA: Tell me all about it.

MAMA: It was the happiest day of my life.

LYOSHA: Was it love at first sight?

PAPA hesitates

MAMA: Of course it was.

LYOSHA: Where did you meet?

PAPA: Your mum and I were at the same school.

MAMA: It was at the funfair, wasn't it Kostya? I was with my class going on the rides. And Kostya was there with his class. And we were queueing for the merry-go-round. And

Daddy was queuing for the roller coaster, even though the teacher had said we couldn't go on that.

LYOSHA: Why not?

PAPA: Dangerous. One little boy fell out of his car and they never even found his body. Just his lunchbox.

MAMA: Daddy came over to our class and said, who's going on the roller coaster then? And everyone else was too scared, but I said yes, because I'd liked your daddy for a long time and he hadn't even noticed me.

PAPA: Oh that's not fair. I had. I thought, what a big nose that girl's got.

MAMA: (*With pity.*) Well I hadn't seen all your shortcomings at that point. So me and him, we ran away from all the others. He bought the tickets and we climbed right up to the top. There wasn't a lift then. And they used to pull the cars up by hand. And then this enormous drop right down and then up again and again and again…

LYOSHA: And you weren't scared?

MAMA: If I had known your father a little better I would have been. But no, I felt as safe as houses.

PAPA: And who wet their pants?

MAMA: Liar!

She flicks him with the dirty sheet. LYOSHA laughs in delight.

LYOSHA: And then?

MAMA: Then we went shooting down on the roller coaster and we felt suddenly very close. I bought Daddy some ice cream and we had a ride on the merry-go-round and hid from the teachers and the rest of the kids. We had such good fun. And then it rained.

LYOSHA: Was it summer?

PAPA: No, it was spring.

MAMA: Are you sure?

PAPA: Of course I am. It was April. The chestnut trees weren't even in flower.

MAMA: Why weren't we at school then?

PAPA: It was a holiday.

MAMA: Well, I don't know. For some reason I thought it was the end of May.

PAPA: You just have to argue, don't you? I don't remember the date but it was the day the reactor blew up.

MAMA: That's right! I remember now! You're right.

PAPA: Finally.

MAMA: We all got drenched in the rain. Daddy held his wet shirt over me to shelter me. Do you remember?

PAPA: And when we got home we heard on TV that there had been an accident at the nuclear plant. And the rain was radioactive rain.

MAMA: (*Blissfully.*) That's right. That's what happened. I flew home – on the wings of love! You kissed me on the cheek. I remember thinking, I must remember this day. This is the happiest day of my life. Remember?

PAPA: I didn't kiss you on the cheek – I french-kissed you. Are you trying to humiliate me in front of my son?

LYOSHA listens happily to his parents.

LYOSHA: And then what?

PAPA: Then what? Well, everything just kept getting better. All the schools in Kiev were shut down and the kids were sent to camps all over the place. Some went to the sea, to the Crimea, some to Moscow. And we were treated like kings everywhere. No school, no exams.

MAMA: We had a whole four months holiday, instead of the usual three. Everyone came back taller, more grown up, suntanned. And it was completely free. Some kids were even sent abroad for treatment.

LYOSHA: Cool! And what happened then?

PAPA: Well son, then we all came back to Kiev in September and things took their usual course. Your mum and I carried on seeing each other. Then we left school and went on to institute and then we got married and then we got divorced... Just like everyone else.

LYOSHA: And when did I appear?

MAMA: Later. When we got married again.

LYOSHA: Why? Didn't it work first time round?

PAPA: It rarely does first time round.

LYOSHA: What was it like, Mum?

MAMA: What?

LYOSHA: How did you make me?

MAMA: Well... It was... (*To her husband, quietly.*) You tell him. But don't mention the vodka.

PAPA: Well, you see, your mother and I separated for six months.

LYOSHA: Why?

MAMA: Your father was very badly behaved towards me.

PAPA: I thought you didn't want to tell him?

MAMA: No, you'd better. 'Cause once I get started…

PAPA: Anyway, your mother left me. Because she was stupid. I rang and rang but she put the phone down on me. Hated me, I suppose.

MAMA: Well that's true. I hated you.

PAPA: So she hated me although I was suffering without her. I thought I'd be alright, I'd pull through, but I wasn't.

MAMA gloats.

I kept meaning to go and see her, but I didn't have the cash for champagne. And I felt a bit awkward arriving without the champagne and the flowers. But happily, just when things were getting really bad, and I almost died without your mum, there was that incident with the skyscrapers.

LYOSHA: What skyscrapers?

PAPA: (*Indignant.*) What do they teach you at school, Lyosha?

MAMA: The poor kid's been in hospitals for the last three years.

PAPA: Right, well, it was when some aeroplanes crashed into some skyscrapers.

LYOSHA: Wow! Straight into the skyscrapers? At top speed?

PAPA: They showed it on every TV channel. It was amazing! And I thought to myself, well it's now or never. She won't chase me away on a day like today. So I bought a bottle of vodka…

MAMA: (*Sarcastically.*) Thanks for that.

PAPA: Oh come on. He's a man, he understands these things. So anyway, I bought a bottle of vodka and I went to see your mum and I said, 'Lyuda, on a day like today we should be together. All our problems are nothing compared to this tragedy. Look – there are people dying in terrorist attacks and all you can think of are those girls I once… Anyway, you can forgive someone their infidelities and put things right if they are still alive, but up there in that skyscraper there's no putting anything right. Forgive me, Lyuda. Let's get married again.' That's what I said. I put it well, I did.

LYOSHA: What about you?

MAMA: They kept showing this picture on TV of a man sheltering a woman from the bits of rubble falling from the Trade Centre and I suddenly felt such gratitude towards that man – that I forgave your father.

PAPA: And I went and bought a second bottle of vodka.

LYOSHA: And then what happened?

MAMA: And then you were born. Nine months later. What a happy coincidence.

LYOSHA: And what about the skyscrapers? Did they all fall down?

PAPA: No, no, only two of them. But they've built some new ones there now. Whenever we see them we remember that day.

LYOSHA: Can you go there?

MAMA: 'Course you can. Climb on a plane and in eight hours you're in New York. Wonderful.

LYOSHA: And Chernobyl?

PAPA: Even easier. It's no distance at all. They run day-trips down there. It only takes two hours on a bus to reach the Zone. It's very nice down there at the moment. Your mum and I were planning a trip at the weekend. Your mother could do with the fresh air.

MAMA strokes her stomach.

LYOSHA: How did you make her?

MAMA and PAPA exchange glances.

MAMA: Well what happened nine months ago?

PAPA: What happened? A government coup. We were celebrating and forgot the contrac– (*Interrupts himself.*)

LYOSHA: The what?

MAMA: Nothing. We decided that the time had come to give you a little sister.

LYOSHA: Thanks. So will you take me and my sister to Chernobyl?

MAMA: Of course.

LYOSHA: Will you take me there when I'm better?

MAMA: Of course we will. But you won't get better unless you eat up your chicken soup.

LYOSHA: With onion?

MAMA: All the onion's gone. Daddy ate it. I'll pour you a cup.

LYOSHA: And I'll get better?

MAMA: Definitely.

LYOSHA: (*With heroic obedience.*) Go on then.

MAMA pours soup into a cup. LYOSHA, overcoming his revulsion, eats.

PAPA: That's my boy!

LYOSHA: I want everything to be as great for me as it has been for you.

MAMA: Everything will be wonderful. And even better than for us. We'll do everything we can. (*Carefully.*) But you must be prepared for life's little storms as well, love.

MAMA starts collecting up her things.

LYOSHA: (*Scared.*) You're not leaving are you? Don't go…

MAMA: We must. It's very late. Grandma's on her own at home. I've got to make dinner and feed the fish. Take the dog for a walk. You should see the dog, Lyosha, how it's grown. Eats like a horse!

PAPA: Your mother needs her sleep just at the moment.

MAMA and PAPA kiss LYOSHA in turn.

LYOSHA: Are you coming tomorrow?

MAMA: Of course we are, sweetheart.

LYOSHA: In the morning?

MAMA: We can't do the morning, Lyosha. Your dad has work and I've got to go to the clinic. We'll come after lunch.

PAPA: I need to earn the money to pay for this treatment of yours.

LYOSHA cries.

LYOSHA: Please come a bit earlier. Please.

PAPA: Alright. I'll take time off work and come early morning when you're still asleep. You'll wake up and I'll be sitting here. Don't cry Lyosha, be a man.

LYOSHA: I'm not a man! I'm not! I'm not!

His parents glance nervously at each other.

LYOSHA tries not to cry.

MAMA: That's my boy. Now go to sleep and have some sweet dreams.

LYOSHA quietens and his parents tiptoe out of the ward.

LYOSHA: They left on tiptoe, as if I was asleep. Stupid. I'm not going to sleep. I'm sad, all alone like this in the hospital. I'd really like to get up out of bed and go home with Mum and Dad. But I can't because I'm ill. I could try, I suppose, while no one's looking. There, see. I can do it. I'm getting up out of bed and I'm walking out of the ward. How easy. The nurses are all asleep around the table. I'm the little invisible boy from a fairy tale, slipping past the guards. I walk through the night in my seven-league boots, and I'm full of strength and joy like my dad. Think how surprised they'll be! And here is my beautiful red-brick house. Nothing has changed, my toy box is where I left it – but full of new toys. But Djinn the dog won't let me play – he wants me to come out with him. We go into the yard – and look, he's turned into a little horse! I can ride him! We gallop across the green meadows, me holding on tight to Djinn's ears. Now we are on the roller coaster, going down into a beautiful valley called Chernobyl. There's a garden full of enormous flowers – daisies and roses, and Mum and Dad are coming out to meet us, but they look tiny next to the huge flowers. Beautiful couples are wandering in the garden, drinking vodka, and their tummies are growing and out of them come tumbling babies like me. And now we are soaring over the high green grass. Djinn is a plane now – look, Mum! Look, Dad! We're flying over a city. And now we crash into skyscrapers and they fall apart into millions of beautiful red bricks. My parents are happy. They'll never argue again! And that's the most important thing in my life. Me and my parents. The most important thing. Where are they? I want to fly back to Mum and Dad and the valley called Chernobyl – but we are flying over a sea of chicken soup. Don't fall into the soup – it's got onion in it! How huge this sea is! Djinn! Something's gone wrong with the plane! We're falling! I'm scared! It can't happen to me! To someone else, but not me! I'm too small to die like everyone else. Am I dreaming? I must be, I can't feel any hurt from falling. I can feel a pillow under my head. I'm in hospital. How happy I am. Papa... Is it you already?

PAPA: I told you I'd be here when you woke up.

LYOSHA: I was flying and then falling. Flying and falling. It was nice at first and then it was scary.

PAPA: Don't be scared. It means you're growing up.

PAPA drinks beer and looks tenderly at the sleepy LYOSHA.